The Fearless Boy

The Detractor And The Glutton

Daniel Ndubuisi Nnerdy

Copyright ©2018 DNN International
Published by Daniel Nnerdy
dnnerdy.1@gmail.com
+ 234 7060419778
ISBN: 9781717752055

DNN International Edition License Notes

This ebook is licensed for your personal enjoyment only. This ebook may not be re-sold or given away to other people. If you would like to share this book with another person, please purchase an additional copy for each recipient. If you're reading this book and did not purchase it, or it was not purchased for your enjoyment only, then please return to DNN International or your favorite retailer and purchase your own copy. Thank you for respecting the hard work of this author.

Preface

A superb short story with an obvious evidence of verisimilitude. It's a didactic short story that one must have a copy and another for his or her generation.   The fearless boy is an antidote to the ravaging societal ills in our youths now days. The fearless boy and other stories in majority narrates of a young growing boy who wasted his glorious life and later realized that the only way of surviving and being reckoned with in the society is to be educated.   So you can find out how the fearless boy went astray, but later found the direct part to success.

Dedication

This book is dedicated to youths who wish to become great in future.

Contents

Daniel Ndubuisi Nnerdy

Acknowledgements

My acknowledgements to all those who contributed immensely to see that this book is published, I pray may God grant each and every one of you your heart desire.

CHAPTER ONE
The Troublesome Boy

Obinze was the youngest child and the only son of Chief Ubani and Madam Ifemelue in Nnewi town of Anambra State. His parents had given birth to five female children before he was born. Since he had been born, his parents never had peace of mind again. He grew up to become more stubborn, aggressive, offensive and rude. He never obeyed anybody at home, in the school, in their village and even in the church. When he was six years old, his parents organized a birthday party for him.

During the arty, he fought with a boy because he did not dance well. He called the boy all sorts of bad names and when the boy's parents complained, Obinze refused to apologize. Instead, he told them to take the boy away or else he would beat him again. Surprisingly, when his father intervened, he told him to stay out of it because it was none of his business.

There was nothing Obinze could not say, there was nobody he could not challenge or insult. Many times, he would challenge his sister's authority at home. One day, they were going to the farm and his eldest sister, Chinasa, gave him a knock on the head because he was walking too slowly.

Obinze did not say anything because a plan for revenge was brewing at the back of his mind. No sooner had they started working on the farm than he threw a stone which hit Chinasa on the forehead. The stone caused an injury and she bled profusely. She was immediately rushed to the village health Centre by passersby, where the bleeding was urgently attended to and her forehead was also stitched.

Later that night, Obinze was expected to return home but he refused to come home because he knew he would be severely dealt with by his no-nonsense father. By seven p.m., he was yet to be home. And so when it was 9:30pm, his parents, already worried to death, decided to turn themselves to hunters in search of Obinze. They searched every nook and cranny of the house and the streets but he was nowhere to be found. When it was 11:pm, they gave up the search and agreed to go back to sleep with the view of continuing their search the following day.

As they got to the house, Obinze's mother instinctively decided to look up in the direction of the cashew tree in front of the house. When Madam Ifemelu lit the tree with the torch in her hand, she saw Obinze where he perched precariously on one of the branches. They had to beg him before he agreed to come down and before he came down, he had told them that no one must neither beat him nor scold him.

That night, they all went inside quietly and slept without verbally abusing him and he refused to eat the food given to him. The following day when he was coming back from school, he saw some middle-aged boys that were playing football. One of them unintentionally played the ball towards his direction and the ball hit him.

Without further ado, Obinze took the ball and burst it with a long nail he had with him. These boys pounced on him like a hungry lion on its prey. They beat him mercilessly and left him on the playground. Obinze managed to get home with his swollen lips. On getting home, his mother shouted and went to the playground but the boys had already taken to their heels.

Chinasa and Amaka, his second sister, held his hands while their mother massaged his lips and other parts of his body. With the injury sustained, one would think that Obinze would change his immoral attitude and behave like a responsible son since he had met his doom. That was not the case with Obinze because, whether pounded in a mortar or ground on a grinding stone, pepper will remain inseparable. While his lips were massaged, he still scolded Amaka because he thought she was mocking him with her cackling laughter.

CHAPTER TWO
Obinze In Church

Obinze never stopped amazing people in the village and he was fond of taking people aback with his mode of dressing. On Sunday he went to church and when it was time to give the offering in the children's department, Obinze refused to drop the twenty naira which his father had given at home. The evangelist in charge of the children's department of the church called him and asked why he refused to give his offering.

"I didn't feel like giving," he replied boldly.

Some minutes later, Obinze fought with Godwin because he had refused to share his biscuit with him. He pushed Godwin, and he hit his forehead on the ground. Immediately, Godwin was rushed to the pastor's quarters. Obinze was told to kneel down until the adults ended their service. The Evangelist reported him to the Senior Pastor and he also told him that Obinze refused to give his offering.

"To begin with, why didn't you give your offering?" The pastor inquired.

"Because 1 didn't feel like paying; besides you have always been the only one spending the money all this while. Therefore, I'm tired of paying," he replied with a nonchalant attitude.

The pastor stood aghast because the response stunned him. The pastor told him to fast for just one day to seek forgiveness from God but he would stay in the church. Obinze blatantly refused what the pastor told him and went home without permission, leaving his parents behind. Godwin's parents were infuriated by Obinze's reaction.

"Chief Ubani, if not for your integrity and the power thrusted on you as a chief, 1 know what 1 would have done. Nevertheless, you are not responsible enough for not teaching your son the right thing", Godwin's father said angrily.

"It's not your fault" Madam Ifemelu intoned. Chief Ubani felt humiliated by Godwin's father's comment about him yet he pretended as if he did not hear him. The pastor settled everything amicably and implored Chief Ubani and Madam Ifemelu to train their son properly so that he could give them peace of mind. They left the pastor's quarters for their residence.

At home, Obinze was at the front of the house, playing with his "rubber band" with some boys. Initially he pretended as if he did not see his parents.

"Obinze didn't you see us?" His father asked.

"I did, but as you can see, I am playing a game with my friends and I must defeat them before I go in because they've defeated me three times and if I don't win, I may fight again and I know you wouldn't want me to fight, would you?" he said. Madam Ifemelu wanted to beat him for being rude but his father stopped her. They entered the house quietly.

Obinze did not enter the house throughout the day because his mindset was that he would be decisively dealt with. Therefore, when he observed that everybody was asleep, he sneaked in. By midnight, his father entered his room with the sole aim of advising him. After speaking with him for some minutes, his father finally said. "Obinze my son, no undisciplined person has ever become great. In this sense, if you don't listen to what your parents are telling you, you will perish".

"I'll change," he said remorsefully.

In the morning, Obinze astonished everybody. He fetched water and also washed some dirty plates before he left for school. At school, he behaved well for the first time and for the very first time, he was not late. When the school closed, he went home directly without joining other boys to play football. At home, he fetched water, washed plates and also washed his uniform. He didn't go out to play neither did he cause any trouble.

Without being informed, he did his homework and sought his sister's assistance where necessary. Everybody was happy because of his good behaviour for the day, but no one knew what would ensue next day.

CHAPTER THREE
The Masquerade Festival

It was masquerade festival, everybody was at the market square to see masquerades and also watch some women that danced to traditional songs. Earlier oh, some boys had wrestled among themselves to know the strongest boy in the community. After all the performances, the king addressed everybody and urged them to continue to co-exist peacefully. The king along with his chiefs left for the palace while old men and women returned home. However, children were left at the market square chanting different eulogies after the masquerades.

The masquerades were of different sizes and height. When Obinze was tired of chanting, he decided to return home. On his way home, he saw a masquerade which was of the same height with him. The masquerade told Obinze to give him money or else he would not let Obinze go home but Obinze refused.

"I thought you are not a beggar". He said. The masquerade nodded his head in acceptance to what Obinze said. "Therefore, leave the road now and let me go home before l crunch you", Obinze warned the masquerade. When the masquerade refused to let go of him, Obinze pushed him away but the masquerade stood up immediately and held his cloth. This infuriated him, so he slapped the masquerade and they began to fight. Before old people mover closer to the scene, Obinze had torn the masquerade's garment and ran away.

However, when he got home, he told his mother what he did and she shouted.

"Haa! You this boy has finally implicated me". His mother said. When his father returned, he was also told about what happened. He opened his mouth in shock. His mother and his sister were worried about very soon the council of elders would come to their house to take him to the shine for his punishment. As they were still contemplating over what to do, a woman hurriedly ran into their house. They were scared when they saw her.

"What happened and why did you barge in like that?" Madam Ifemelu inquired.

"Chief, chief, if you like your son, take him out of this house now because the elders are coming here to take him to the shrine and he will be killed immediately"!   She spoke gaspingly. "But the punishment is grievous at least both of us should be punished because the masquerade caused everything. If he had allowed me to go, 1 wouldn't have fought with him. That's injustice". Obinze said smugly.

"Shut up. You this bastard now go in there and pack your belongings. You are going to stay with my sister in Obosi until everything is settled," his father said.   After some minutes of argument, Obinze packed his clothes and Chinasa was instructed to take him to their Auntie's house in Obosi.

Barely had they left when the council of elders arrived. "Chief Ubani where is your son, Obinze?"   One of the elders requested. "We've not seen him since morning; 1 guess he must still be at the market square", Madam Ifemelu lied. "We give you just two hours to bring your son to us", the elders said in unison.

The council of elders returned to the chief Ubani's house later, but they were told that Obinze had run away from home and they had not been able to reach him since he had left home. However, because of Chief Ubani's integrity in the town, the council of elders said they had forgiven him therefore Obinze could now return to Nnewi.

CHAPTER FOUR
Discipline In School

In Obosi, Obinze was enrolled into S.S.S. 1 in Community High School. Initially, he tried to hide his behaviour, but it could not be hidden. He never tolerated nonsense from his classmates. Obinze was well-known in the school, he would not come out to join the morning assembly and when it was sports period, he would not be seen among the students.

Obinze had formed a new gang in the school so during the morning devotion and also during sports periods, they would go and hide behind the school garden where they would be hunting rats and other small animals. One day, Mr. Onazi, the English teacher, beat Obinze because he did not do his assignment. Obinze felt humiliated in the presence of his classmates and so, he decided to revenge. During the break-time, Obinze broke the windscreen of Mr. Onazi's Volkswagen car. He was very happy to have done such evil to the teacher.

At the end of the academic session, Ngozi, the class teacher's daughter came first in the class and it was obvious to every student that Nkechi was the most outstanding student in the class. Nevertheless, Obinze told the students that they were going to protest and he volunteered to lead the students round the school premises and they would settle everything in the principal's office. While protesting, they were singing different songs such as: "We no go gree ooo, we no go gree ooo, lai, lai, lai we no go gree". The teachers and other students were just looking at them as they marched peacefully to the principal's office.

The principal came out of his office immediately he heard their voices. "Alright, what's the meaning of this, what do you want?" The principal asked. "Thank you sir, we know in our class that Nkechi is the most brilliant student, although we are also intelligent, Nkechi outshines us". He enthused.
"If l may ask…"

"What's your own position, Obinze", the principal asked. "Well, we are all leaders but some leaders are supreme to others. So my position is 75th," he said. "And how many of you are in the class", the principal asked again.

"We are just 80 in the class and at least, l have five behind me, "he replied.

"So, why are you protesting?"

"We are protesting because our class teacher changed the result because of his daughter". Before the principal could say anything, they had turned back and gone to their classroom. The following session when the school resumed, Obinze who was fond of coming late to school met his waterloo on Monday morning. One of the prefects at the gate challenged him for coming late and instead of pleading guilty; he was bragging and promised to deal with the prefects if they touched him. These prefects, who had heard more of Obinze's arrogance, pounced on him and beat him to a pulp. As if that was not enough, the prefects reported him to the school principal.

A little later, the principal called him out at the assembly. "Every one of you should listen to me carefully; Community High School is not a haven for criminals and undisciplined students. Any student that thinks he is too big to be trained or punished here should stay at home. Without mincing words, Obinze Obidiegwu, you are hereby suspended from this school for three weeks, but before you go, l will teach you a lesson you will never forget". Principal said with a harsh voice.

The principal called the senior boy and some male prefects to carry Obinze so that he could flog him properly. Afterwards, Obinze carried his bag and went home. On his way home, he felt the pain on his buttocks while his mind was full of arsenic thoughts. He thought about how he would return to school and was also soliloquizing about what to tell his aunty at home.

Obinze told his aunty that he been temporarily suspended from the school for three weeks. Aunty Ifeoma welcomed the idea wholeheartedly without condemning the principal's decision. Obinze was furious by aunty Ifeoma's reaction to his suspension but there was nothing he could do.

CHAPTER FIVE
Tied To The Stake

Obinze had no cut out plan for his life, so the thought of how to become prosperous in life was far from him. He met his doom again when he went to peep at a woman, Rita, while she was bathing in the bathroom. He had been there for some minutes without any sign that he would leave there. Suddenly, he was beaten from behind. He wanted to talk, but when he looked up, he found out that it was Rita's husband, so he kept mute. Rita was surprised when her husband told her what Obinze did.

He was seriously dealt with as if he was a thief. He pleaded seriously but all his efforts were thwarted by Mama Henry who told them to deal with him very well because that's how he always peeped at women whenever they were bathing. Obinze confessed that he had seen Rita's nakedness many times. On hearing this, Rita pounced on him and bit him. By now, many people were at the scene making all sorts of negative comments about him. Obinze had no friend on the street. No parent wanted their child to associate with him because of his behaviour. He had fought with everybody and once embarrassed the king.

One day, the king was passing by and Obinze refused to greet him. "Young boy can't you greet or am 1 too small to be seen by you?" The king challenged him.

"Must 1 greet everyone that 1 see?" He shrugged. The king was humiliated by his response. No one could come to his aid except his aunty and she was not around. Rita ran inside as if she had run mad, she came out with a bottle of kerosene and one pack of match sticks.

"Please 1 won't do it again". Obinze said ruefully. "Lynch him that serves him right". Mama Henry said.

Rita had poured the kerosene on him and her husband wanted to set him ablaze when an old woman appealed to them to apply another strategy to deal with him. Obinze was relieved when he realized that he would not be lynched. Rita's husband brought out a stake and a very long strong rope. Obinze was tied to the stake and little children were making fun of him because Rita and her husband had his cloth stripped him naked.

"Please give me water, 1 am thirsty" Obinze pleaded.

"No water for you, you'll die of thirst" Rita's husband said.

"Honey, 1 suggest we give him water so that he doesn't die here" Rita said fearfully.

"He can't die, that water will only make him stronger". He said Aunty Ifeoma was very worried at home because she had not seen the troublesome boy since morning. Everyone was standing outside expecting Obinze's arrival. When it was 9:30pm and Obinze was yet to be at home, they all went inside but Aunty Ifeoma's husband decided to search for him.

As he was going, he heard somebody groaning in pain and moved closer to the person. He was amazed when he found out that it was Obinze. He untied him and carried him home. On getting home, he managed to have his bath and refused to answer every question that he was asked and he did not eat before he slept off.

CHAPTER SIX
War At Home

Obinze had now stopped doing house chores. He felt too big to carry a bucket of water on his head; he could no longer wash plates, neither could he assist his auntie's husband on the farm. Obinze here and Obinze there, he was more feared than "Boko-Haram". One day, he beat Aunty Ifeoma's daughter, Chioma because she advised him to be serious. "Obinze, l pity you. You better strike when the iron is hot.

Very soon you will be writing your final Secondary School Examination and you are not reading", she said with concern. Obinze pretended as if he did not hear what she said. He continued peeling an orange. Chioma continued advising him as if she was his mother.

"Obinze, your mates are doing great things out there, some of them have a vegetable farm. Here you are, doing nothing, absolutely nothing. Fighting every day, causing trouble every day, no respect for the elders and…"
"Shut up!" He shouted.

The head that's destined to receive knock on the head will surely receive it even if locked inside, it will peep out through the window. Chioma did not stop advising Obinze in a sarcastic manner. When Obinze could not endure it again, he stood up and beat Chioma like a snake.

He beat her to his own satisfaction before he left her. Chioma reported him to her mother when she entered and aunty Ifeoma asked him the reason why he dealt with chioma. Obinze said Chioma was rude to him and he decided to punish her.

"So she was rude for advising you", Aunty Ifeoma said. "Are you trying to say l can't deal with my sister if she misbehaves to me?" He asked. Aunty Ifeoma was very angry with Obinze's reaction. She beat him with her palms but Obinze was trying to prevent her hand from touching him.

"No supper for you in this house today", Aunty Ifeoma said, as she left for the kitchen. Later in the night, Obinze sneaked into the kitchen and stole the food he saw there. He ate the food and returned the plates to its previous position as if nothing happened. When Aunty Ifeoma's husband got home, he requested for his food. Aunty Ifeoma entered the kitchen with the aim of giving her husband his food, not knowing that Obinze had eaten it. "Haa, Obinze, Obinze, Obinze", she shouted his name.

"Yes aunty," he answered for his room. "Come over here! Where is the food that l kept in the kitchen for my husband?" She asked angrily.

"Is that why you shouted my name as if l fainted? Anyway l didn't see any food and henceforth, if you want to call me, call me with a very calm voice", he responded nonchalantly. Before he finished his statement, Aunty Ifeoma, with lightning speed, closed the gap between them in one leap and landed a dirty slap on his face. She wanted to do it again and again but her husband prevented her from causing serious damage to Obinze's red face. She also wanted to hit him with a stick that was used to prop the door but Obinze wisely dodged it.

At last, Aunty Ifeoma's husband was able to restore peace and told them to sit down. He admonished Obinze and urged him to change his attitude if he really wanted to become great.

Finally, he asked Obinze what he would have eaten if he had not bought fried yam and potato from where he went to. All that Obinze could say was, "Sorry sir, l will change".

CHAPTER SEVEN
Obinze Fail

It's the end of the journey at Community High School. students were now writing their final secondary school examination. One would wonder what Obinze wrote down as answers because he did not have a single notebook, not to mention reading. He turned deaf ears to the advice given to him. The School Principal had always told them to read their books.

"My dear students please read you books and get yourselves fully prepared for the examination. Don't think that you will be assisted during the examination. If you think that mannah will fall and mannah refuses to fall, what will you do?"

Mannah in this sense was "expo". Obinze was one of the students that did not prepare for the examination. During the examination, he did all that he could do and waited patiently for the outcome of the examination.

Some months later, the result was released but Obinze Failed woefully. When he saw his result, he nearly fainted. When he regained his senses, Chioma mocked him and even invited some of her friends to do the same.

"English Language – F9, Mathematics – F9, Economics – F9, Literature – F9, Commerce – F9, Government – F9, Biology – F9, Agric-Science – D7 and Igbo-Language – D7. What a good result", Chioma teased.

Obinze fell sick for some days. When he recovered, he decided to return to his parents because the stigma in OBOSI was too much for him to bear. Before he left, Aunty Ifeoma called him and encouraged him not to lose hope. "Obinze, the downfall of a man is not the end of his life. Do not lose hope; you can still make it as long as you are ready to rectify your mistakes. Remember that it is not what happens to you that determine how far you go in life; it is what you do with what happens to you".

"Therefore, since you've said that you are going back to your parents, 1 wish you well. Great your parents for me. Safe journey", she added. Aunty Ifeoma gave him some money, Obinze thanked her and hugged Chioma. Eventually, he carried his bag and left for

Nnewi.

Obinze got home and narrated his ordeal to his parents. His mother pitied him but his father did not. All his sisters had made progress. Chinasa and Amaka had graduated from the University while his other three sisters had also been offered admission into the University. Obinze was depressed because of his failure. Later in the evening, his father called him under the cashew tree and started encouraging him.

"Binze my son, 1 know you have learnt you lesson and you wish you had listened to your parents and your teachers. Nevertheless, since you have realized your mistakes and are ready to rectify them, there is no problem. It is just that one year has been wasted from your years. Next year you ought to go to the University, but now, you will have to stay in the Secondary School for an extra year. Well, yours will serve as a lesson to other stubborn children like you"! Chief Ubani said.

Tears rolled down his checks briskly. He wanted to talk but he could not. Within two days, the news that Obinze had returned had spread round the town, "wahala don come back again" some said while some mocked him because they'd heard that he failed his examination. Obinze could not walk freely anymore. He was very disappointed when he found out that most of his friends passed the examination and they would be going to the university soon. The stigma was too much for him.

One day, one of his uncles, Chidi, who lived in Lagos came to Nnewi for a burial ceremony. After the ceremony, Obinze appealed to his uncle to take him along to Lagos because he could no longer bear the embarrassment.

"There is just one Obinze, no other, and they only one that 1 know is troublesome and fearless. So, 1 can't take him to Lagos because the boys in Lagos are more fearless and troublesome than he is", his uncle said. After some minutes, his uncle agreed to his demand. Obinze was very happy. He ran inside to pack his things in a disorganized manner.

Chief Ubani and Madam Ifemelu thanked Chidi for accepting to take their son to Lagos. The following morning, Obinze woke up as early as possible, he wore a black shirt with "Why always me" inscription on it. When Chidi was about to leave for Lagos, he gave some money to the old people and also gave something to each of the children in the house.

At this time, Obinze was already seated majestically at front seat of the car. Some minutes later, Chidi entered the car and began to drive off. Chief Ubani and Madam Ifemelu waved at them until it was out of sight.

CHAPTER EIGHT
New Life In Lagos

Chidi and his wife together with their two children lived in a two bedroom apartment in Lagos. He had a shop where foodstuffs were sold. He was well known in Obawole Because he had been selling foodstuffs there for many years.

The day after Obinze got to Lagos, Chidi took him to his shop with the view of showing him how to sell the foodstuffs and how to attend to the consumers. "Obinze, you must make sure you attend to the consumers very well, don't abuse them or insult them although they may be silly at times. Chidi instructed Obinze with a very calm voice.

On the third day, Chidi went to his second shop at Haruna while Obinze began his new life in the first shop. Obinze would open the shop by 7:30am and close at 9:00pm daily. He quickly adapted with the system and the customers loved him, even "the street boys" because they often used his shop as a venue to analysis some sporting issues every morning.

Obinze continued his life in the shop and in his uncle's house for so many years without thinking about education. His uncle gave him ten thousand naira monthly and he also realized at least one thousand naira daily.

He thought he was a big boy because he used a nice phone and he could provide his girlfriend's basic needs. The whole story changed suddenly when Chima came to buy foodstuff at the shop. Chima also hailed from Nnewi. He was the boy whose ball was burst by Obinze when Obinze was coming back from school.

Chima now had his company in Lagos. He had built his house the previous year and also married a pretty lady. Obinze did not recognize him again but the memory of how Obinze burst the ball and how Chima and his playmates ha pounced on Obinze was very fresh in Chima's memory.

"Hello, excuse me. Aren't you Obinze? Chima asked.

"I am."

"Don't you recognize me anymore?" he asked again.

"I don't know you sir," Obinze replied respectfully. "But you're Chief Ubani's son in Nnewi", Chima added.

"He even know my father's name and my town", Obinze soliloquized. "I am Chima, the then small boy who you burst his ball at the playground in Nnewi" Chima explained. Obinze opened his mouth in astonishment, he was surprised to see Chima and at the same time, he was ashamed of himself when Chima told him that the car he came with belonged to him.

"Is this your shop?" Chima inquired. "No, it's not mine. It belongs to my uncle", Obinze replied. "Okay, but this is not the right place for us to talk", Chima said. Chima gave him his complimentary card and told him to call him anytime he wanted to come and see him in his office. Obinze was completely taken aback again when Chima gave his card to him.

"He is even the CEO of Chi and Sons Limited in Opebi", Obinze muttered. Chima paid for the foodstuffs and gave Obinze two thousand naira to transport himself to his office after that he entered his car and drove off slowly.

Throughout that day, Obinze did not feel fine, he wasn't happy and he felt disappointed within himself. When he got home, he only managed to eat his supper and explained how things went in the shop to his uncle. Obinze could not sleep because he was recounting his wasted years as a wayward boy. "Had 1 known, 1 would have faced my studies and become prosperous", he said to himself. He stomped his foot on the floor every second and bit his fingers in regret as tears rolled down his face briskly.

The following day was Thursday which was an environmental day for market men and women in Lagos State. Obinze quickly went to the shop in the morning to do some cleaning and told his uncle that he wanted to go to Opebi to see one of his friends. Uncle Chidi allowed him to go because he had never sought such permission before. He wore Christiana Ronaldo's Real Madrid white jersey and a blue pair of jeans. Although Obinze was a Chelsea fan, he loved Ronaldo very dearly.

Obinze couldn't believe what his eyes saw and what he witnessed in Chima's office. He was delayed for some minutes at the gate before he was allowed to enter the reception. At the reception, the receptionist told him to fill the visitor's register before he could be allowed to see Chima.

Having filled the register, Obinze still sat at the reception for fifteen minutes before he finally spoke out. "Please when is it going to be my turn to see Chima?" he asked the receptionist who pretended not to hear what he was saying. "Young lady, 1 am talking to you" he said.

"Chu, so it's our boss that you just called like that; you can't see him today because of your disrespectfulness". She said. Obinze stood up and started shouting at the receptionist. It took the intervention of Chima to restore normalcy. "Obinze, what happened?" Chima asked.

He explained all that happened to Chima and when Chima asked the receptionist the reason for delaying Obinze, she said: "He lacks manner of approach and he is not well dressed". Without much ado, Chima took Obinze to his well-furnished office. "Guy you don do well for yourself oo", Obinze said with a glint in his eyes. "Bross na God dey do am oo", Chima replied.

Obinze kept quiet for some seconds while Chima received a call.

"So why didn't you finish your education or don't you know the importance of education?" Chima asked brusquely. Obinze was speechless, or rather; he didn't know what to say. "My brother, 1 know the value of education but 1 missed my path, 1 mean 1 failed woefully. Therefore, 1 decided to leave Nnewi for Lagos so that 1 can avoid the embarrassment at home and in our town not knowing that I'll still be humiliated when 1 see someone like you". He said as an afterthought.

"What do you mean by being humiliated?" Chima asked.
"I mean 1 envy those of you that were well-educated. There's no limit to where you can go, talk or sit in the society but for someone like me, there is a limit. What happened in your reception is a good example". Obinze replied with a low voice. His eyes were red, he wanted to cry but he prevented the tears from rolling down his cheeks.

Chima pitied him and told him that he would help him. But Obinze must first help himself by getting himself educated. "Where do you expect me to start, JSS1 or SSS3? For many years, 1 have not read any books not even the popular literary texts such as Things Fall Apart, The Lion and the Jewel, Oliver Twist or Animal Farm. I am twenty-seven years old, next month; I'll be twenty eighty years," Obinze lamented.

Tears were already rolling down his cheeks. He was seriously confused and downcast.

"There are many adults' schools; you can enroll in one of them for some time". Chima said. "There is even one in my area, they call it BRT but where do l start?" "What do you mean by BRT? Chima asked.

"It means Brain Revival Tutors and it is owned and controlled by well-educated tutors" Obinze explained.

"That's good. Go and start in SSS1, if you perform excellently within six months, you will register for the WAEC-GCE. The outcome of that examination will determine the next step to be taken". Chima said. Obinze nodded his head in acceptance to what Chima said. After the discussion, Chima called one of his drivers to drive Obinze to Allen-Avenue where he could easily board a bus to Ogba. In the car Obinze was pondering on what Chima told him to do.

"Adult education SSS1, hmmm" he thought. He was deep in thought to the extent that the driver had to notify him that he had helped him to stop a bus. Obinze quickly alighted from the car to enter the bus.

CHAPTER NINE
The Success Boy

Obinze told his uncle about his intention to further his education and also sought permission from him to allow him go for tutorial in the evening.

"Obinze! You never cease to amaze me. What school do you still want to attend at this age of yours? You better exercise patience; very soon I give you money to start your own business". His uncle said confidently. Obinze was not discouraged by him. Instead, he enlightened his uncle about the unlimited advantages of education. Later, his uncle agreed that he should go to the tutorial by 4:30pm when Godwin, his first son, returned from school so that he could stay in the shop till 7pm when Obinze would be back. Obinze went to the tutorial on Friday to make enquiries so that he could start on Monday.

He met Doyin and Micheal outside while Festus was teaching mathematics and Tope was collecting the lesson fee from the student. After some minutes of discussion, Tope was called to give Obinze a registration form. Obinze went home sad because he saw the group of young teachers that would be teaching him. The following day, he went to a bookshop to buy some of the recommended texts for literature, as he was about leaving the shop, he saw perpetual, one of his juniors at Community High School, Obosi. They greeted each but perpetual could not believe that Obinze could dress neatly and also talk calmly.

"What are you doing here?"

"I came to buy some books here and what are you also doing here?" Obinze replied. "I'm serving as a corp member in Lagos. I just came to buy a novel here" she said. "Corper Perpetual! It's well. I just want to go back to school".

Perpetual squeezed her face when Obinze told her he wanted to go back to school. "For your post graduate study or what?" "which one be post graduate studies? please, I just want to start from S.S.1" Obinze said jokingly.

"You don't mean it; if you're serious it is never too late. Education is the greatest achievement", Perpetual encouraged him. When Obinze got home, he deleted some of his blackberry contacts from 350 to about 30.

He was very determined to be serious. He really wanted to acquire education for himself. Fortunately, his uncle did not disturb him. He allowed him to study hard.

Obinze started the tutorial on a good note and he continued like that for five months. If not for his stubbornness, Obinze would have been a brilliant student in school, his handwriting was legible and he quickly understood whatever he was taught. When the management of the tutorial discovered that Obinze was very serious and determined, he was encouraged to enroll for GCE. "Bros, with what you know and the help of God, you can write GCE and make it", Doyin declared.

"I will think about it and get back to you tomorrow," Obinze said.

When he got home, he called Chima and told him about the registration. "That's good, 1 think those people know better because they are yours teachers" Chima said. "I will register for the examination. Besides, 1 have read all the recommended texts for Literature, 1 think 1 am 50percent prepared," Obinze said courageously. "When will the examination commence?" Chima asked "It begins in September", Obinze replied quickly.

"That means you still have enough time to prepare. We are still in June," Chima said. Obinze registered for the examination and continued with preparation for the examination. His watchword during the examination was "I'll read and get myself prepared, for someday my time will come".

However, because of Obinze's busy schedule, his girlfriend, Adora had left him. Obinze did not reply her message on BBM, did not call her neither did he pick her calls. Examination began very early in September; Obinze's first exam was Biology practical. He did all that he could during the examination and left the rest to the hands of God.

After some months, the result was released. Obinze was very scared but Chima bought the scratch card and checked the result for him. Later in the night, Obinze called Chima to know his fate but Chima did not pick his calls. Obinze had a sleepless night because he had no idea of why Chima did not pick his calls.

Throughout the following day, Chima's phone was switched off. Obinze did not know what to do.

He was in the shop the third day when Chima arrived, Obinze did not laugh at all despite Chima's gestures. "Good day. How is my result?" He asked timidly. Chima gave the result to him with a frown on his face. After some minutes, Obinze jumped up and hugged Chima. "Thank God, thank you Chima. I'm very happy", he said gladly.

"Obinze l am going out. See me in my office tomorrow, we need to discuss." He said and left the shop immediately. The following day in Chima's office, Chima encouraged Obinze to obtain University of Ibadan Distance Learning Form so that he could continue his education and at the same time have the opportunity to secure a better a job while schooling.

Obinze agreed to obtain the form. Chima opened his drawer and gave him fifteen thousand naira. Obinze thanked the form and filled it on the school website. A week later, he received a message from the management that all applicants should prepare for the entrance examination and due to his excellent performance, he was offered admission to study his course of choice-English combined with Communication and Language Arts.

After the payment of the acceptance fees and the school fees, the newly admitted students were matriculated then studying began.

Obinze was well-known in his department, in fact he was appointed as the course representative without any opposition but Obinze was still not happy. He was not happy because he was not where he was supposed to be. He was in the university when his mates were already married.

He would get married when his mates would be reaping the fruit of their labour. "Well, such is life. At least l am finally educated". He said to himself. At the end of the session, Obinze performed brilliantly, with no carry-over or failure. One morning when Obinze was preparing to go to the shop, his phone beeped. When he looked at the screen, he discovered that it was Chima.

"Hello Obinze, please see me at home later in the evening", Chima said sharply. "Okay", Obinze replied. "Only God knows what he wants to see me for". Obinze added as he shut the door. When he closed the shop in the evening, he went to Chima's house.

"Chima, l am here", Obinze said.

"Yes, l just want to tell you that l will need you in my company as my personal assistant with an attractive salary so that you can also start your life." Chima declared. Obinze was quiet. He covered his face with his palms and later wiped his face with them. "Thank you Chima, I'm grateful." He thanked him and wanted to prostrate but Chima prevented from doing so.

Obinze resumed the following week. He wore a well-fitted black suit and a well-polished black Italian shoe. Obinze had already worked for a year when he rented his apartment. He furnished the living room to his own taste. Throughout his time of study at UI DLC, Obinze did not go to Nnewi to visit his parents. He had no fiancé that could distract his attention from his study and his work in Chima's company. He worked assiduously to the extent that Chima handed everything to him and went to London for a vacation. His tenure brought progress to the company. When Chima returned, he rewarded him with a car.

Five years later, Obinze graduated with excellent grades and he was immediate employed as an editor in one of the best national dallies in Nigeria.

Later in December, Obinze presented a precious gift to Chima and his family before he went to Nnewi to celebrate the Christmas with his family but he did not go alone, he went with his fiancé, Chiamaka. Everybody was happy to see him; his sisters also came home to celebrate Obinze's honourable achievement and change of life. They were all seated up and said; "I can't believe this! So l made it at last. I can walk tall and meet those who call me failure and tell them that success has become my other name. although l lost myself before, l have found myself again.

I have learnt my lesson that it doesn't pay to be stubborn. Stubbornness only causes setback in life. Nevertheless, I've realized mistakes." Obinze prostrated before his family members and said, "Thank you, for being there always for me."

CHAPTER TEN
A Dream Unaccomplished

Mr. and Mrs. Akomolafe, together with their two children, were leaving happily before the sudden death of Mr. Akomolafe in a fatal accident. When he was alive, he loved his wife and his children very dearly. In fact, he didn't allow his wife to work or sell anything. But when he died, his family members inherited everything he had worked for and also willed for wife and children. Mrs. Akomolafe was also sent out of the house but she fought hard before she was allowed to take her children along. She rented a room and a parlour from the little money she had in her account and continued to live happily with her children.

A year later, she could not afford the rental charges again therefore she decided to rent one room apartment. One day, Lekan the first child became very sick and Mrs. Akomolafe did not have money to take him to the hospital. She went to her wicked husband's family for assistance but they sent her away like a dog. Unfortunately, Lekan died.

Mrs. Akomolafe was downcast and became depressed. Some weeks after the incident, she decided to start working as a cleaner from house to house so that she would have enough money to cater for her only child, Bukola. Mrs. Akomolafe got three big compounds where she would be paid seven thousand naira monthly apart from that she would also be selling sachet water, sweet and biscuit of different types.

From the little income, she still managed to enroll Bukola into a private nursery and primary school. one day, Bukola was sent back from school because of school fees. She did not go to school for one week so her mother used to take to wherever she wanted to go and sweep.

"Mama Bukola, why was your daughter not been going to school for one week?" Mrs. Anifowoshe the owner of one of the houses she swept asked.

"It's because of her school fees ma", she replied. "When you're through come and see me upstairs. Let me go and discuss with my husband before 1 make any decision," she added. When mama Bukola finished sweeping she went upstairs to see Mrs.

Anifowoshe. "Without mincing words, mama Bukola 1 have discussed with my husband and he has given me permission. If you could permit me, 1 want Bukola to stay with us here as a child so that we can take proper care of her." Mrs. Anifowoshe said.

Mama Bukola knelt down immediately. "I will be grateful ma". "In addition, my husband said he wants you to stop sweeping therefore he said 1 should give you this 10,000 naira so that you use it to support your petty trade although this month salary will be paid." She gave the money to mama Bukola whose joy could not be described as at that moment. She went home gladly leaving Bukola in Mrs. Anifowoshe's house. When she got home, she knelt down and started praising God.

"Thank God, so my daughter will still become an accountant. My child will be greater than Okonjo-Iweala and Sanusi Lamido". She said gratefully. Mama Bukola bought more bags of sachet water and more packets of biscuit and started selling them in front of her house in Ogba, although she still worked as a cleaner in other two houses.

Bukola was well treated.

In fact, anyone who did not know the Anifowoshes before would think Bukola was their biological daughter. When Bukola graduated from primary school, she was also enrolled into the same secondary school that Mrs. Anifowoshe's children were also attending. After some years, Bukola had become a big girl, she would come back late from school and when she got home, she would spend hours making and receiving calls.

Many a time, Mrs. Anifowoshe would call mama Bukola with the view to reporting Bukola's waywardness to her. Some years later when Bukola wrote WAEC, she performed excellently well. Because of the lingering strike in Nigerian universities, Mrs. Anifowoshe promised to send her children and Bukola to go and further their education in Ghana.

She took them to the immigration office for their international passport, and other necessary things. One evening when, Mrs. Anifowoshe and her children together with Bukola was seated in the living room, when mama Jumoke one of the tenants knocked Mrs. Anifowoshe's door.

"Yes come in", Mrs. Anifowoshe said. "Good evening here", Mama Jumoke greeted. "Good evening", everybody in the living room answered her in unison.

"Big mummy, please 1 would like to see you in the verandah", she pleaded. Without any argument, Mrs. Anifowoshe stood up and followed mama Jumoke to the verandah. "Sorry to disturb you ma, have you noticed any changes in your daughter, 1 mean Bukola" she said.
"No, I've not" she replied promptly.

"Bukole is pregnant ma. If you don't know, I've told you. Good night ma", she declared and left immediately. Mrs. Anifowoshe entered the sitting room quickly and told Bukola to see her in her room immediately. When Bukola entered, Mrs. Anifowoshe approached her without dilly dallies. "Bukola, you're pregnant" she said angrily. Bukola was already shivering, she wanted to talk but words wouldn't come out of her mouth.

"Do you know who is responsible for the pregnancy?" she asked.
"Yes ma", Bukola replied.

"That's good; tomorrow you will take me there." The following day, Mr. Anifowoshe drove his wife and Bukola to Oke-Ira where the person was living. When they got there, Bukola alighted from the car and entered a house to call Alomen. Alomen was smoking marijuana when Bukola entered his room. "My parents want to see you outside" she said.

"Your parents, wetin happen, 1 no dem?" he said. Latter he agreed to go and see them outside, Mr. and Mrs. Anifowoshe had already come out of the car. "Good afternoon", Alomen greeted them.

"I greet you well, gentleman", Mr. Anifowoshe replied. "Are you the one who impregnate my daughter" Mrs. Anifowoshe asked. "Your daughter, 1 don't even know any of you before. What kind of rubbish is this? Alomen said. He denied Bukola and blatantly rejected the pregnancy. He did not allow them to say anything again when he had started shouting on them. Mr. and Mrs. Anifowoshe had to leave hurriedly. Immediately they got home, Mrs. Anifowoshe packed all Bukola's belongings and told her to leave her house. She also called mama Bukola to get her informed.

"Hello mama Bukola be expecting your daughter. She is pregnant so 1 have sent her out of my house" she said. "I am finished. this girl had thwarted my dream and also destroyed her future because of five minutes enjoyment", mama Bukola lamented. Some minutes later, Bukola got home and met her mother crying.
She couldn't help crying too.

"Bukola, you have disappointed me and equally embarrassed yourself. L have always proud of you. Now you have disgraced me. Where do 1 want to start from? Who will help me? She wailed. "you have shattered my dreams because 1 can't afford to send you to the polytechnic not to talk of university. I only sell sachet water and biscuit for students.

You were properly placed on the bed but you dragged yourself to the floor. No problem, you will join me in selling water around the street. You will hawk from morning till night and from Monday to Sunday. You will show the pregnancy to everybody so that you can be well humiliated", Mama Bukola finally said. Bukola joined her mother in selling sachet water and they continued living in pain and abject poverty.

CHAPTER ELEVEN
The Detractor And The Glutton

Gbenga and Funke were boarding school students of Obalana High School, Owo, Ondo State. Gbenga was a detractor; there was nobody he could not abuse. Funke on the other hand was a glutton who could eat with a pig. She had always been warned to stop eating whatever she saw so that she would not eat poison.

One day during the drought period, Gbenga placed two of his pocket besides the school well so that he would be the first person to fetch water in the evening, but when students got there in the evening, there was no enough water in the well. In this sense, Gbenga decided to come in the midnight.

When he was about to get to where the well was, he observed that somebody was already fetching water, he was annoyed but he had not known who the person was. Some minutes later, he got there and started talking furiously to the person. He talked for so long, but the person did not reply him. Suddenly, the person turned back to Gbenga it was then that he knew that the person he was abusing was an ogress (a ghost).

He was a bit shocked, but later he summoned courage and started using all sort of derogatory words on the ogress. "I don't care who you're, as long as you met my buckets here; you are not supposed to fetch water before me" he said and pushed the ogress away. Immediately the ogress landed on the floor, she disappeared. Gbenga was scared but after some seconds he fell down. He couldn't stand up and he couldn't talk again. Surprisingly, his tongue began to come out.

When the day finally broke, the first set of students to come and fetch water saw him and quickly went back to call their house master who did not know when and how Gbenga sneaked out of the hostel. When he got there, he was very scared; he couldn't touch him nor move.

The length of the tongue amazed everybody. "This must be 5cm long" Mr. Segun, the house master commented. Gbenga was taken to the school clinic he was immediately transferred to the general hospital before the school management sent for his parents. The doctors treated him for some weeks before they told his parents to take him to a pastor or an herbalist for spiritual treatment. Without much ado, his parents took him to a Celestial Christian Church of God in Akure. Gbenga was there for two months before God finally delivered him.

"I'll never abuse anybody again and 1 will never got out again in the midnight" he promised himself. Funke, on the other hand, was now Adun's bosom friend. Adun was a new student, although she was not a boarder, she would stay in the hostel till 6pm before going home. Adun was the only child of her parents; she was also a witch who had promised her mates that she would return to their fold when she was fifteen years old, not only that she also promised to bring someone along. She brought different types of cake to school for Funke who she knew would definitely eat the cake without asking her for where she got it and even if she asked, Adun would tell her that "My brother is celebrating his birthday, or don't you trust me again?"

So when it was a month to Adun's 15th birthday, she and Funke fell sick. They were taken to different hospital but the entire doctors' efforts to treat them were proved abortive. Five days to Adun's birthday, a pastor who came to pray for the patients in the hospital where Funke was being treated told her parents to bring her to his church because her illness was beyond what they thought. Undisputedly, her parents did what they were told because they had spent a lot of money in the hospital.

In the church, the pastor began serious deliverance for Funke who had partially belonged to the spiritual realm. Some days later, Adun's mother decided to take Adun to a herbalist in Akungba but before they got there, Adun died in the car. Her spirit went to the church where Funke was, thankfully, the pastor had sprinkled Funke with anointing oil.

When the spirit got there, the pastor stood up from where he was seated and began to pray for Funke. He also sprinkled the anointing oil around the church premises before Adun's spirit finally disappeared and Funke began to vomit every cake that Adun had given her. When she was finally delivered, the pastor encouraged her not to always collect gift or food from everybody. Since that day, Funke did not collect food or gift from her friends again because she had learnt a lesson.

The End

Other Books By This Author

Princess Seeks Her Choice Of Husband
Man Known As Iroko Tree
Flurry Sea
The Expected Ones Refuse To Die
Illustrated Stories Of The Ancient Times
Sorrowful Joy

About The Author

Daniel Nnerdy, poet, play writer, novelist and philosopher, studied English and literature at Cocody University in Cote D'Ivoire. Currently in to full time writing, he believes that knowledge redeems society and this is reflected in his writing. He hopes to become a famous writer someday when his writings would help breed the new generation of committed and dedicated leaders in our nation.

About The Book

A superb short story with an obvious evidence of verisimilitude. It's a didactic short story that one must have a copy and another for his or her generation. The fearless boy is an antidote to the ravaging societal ills in our youths now days. The fearless boy and other stories in majority narrates of a young growing boy who wasted his glorious life and later realized that the only way of surviving and being reckoned with in the society is to be educated. So you can find out how the fearless boy went astray, but later found the direct part to success.

www.ingramcontent.com/pod-product-compliance
Lightning Source LLC
Chambersburg PA
CBHW070229260726
48658CB00006BA/2231

9 781717 752055